THE BUSINESS

OF BELIEF

How Your Faith, Willpower,
and Habits Shape Your Success.

PASTOR RASHAWN BEY

The Business of Belief

by PASTOR RASHAWN BEY

Interior Design by One Faith Publishing

Richmond, VA – Port Huron, MI onefaithpublishings@gmail.com

This book or parts thereof may not be reproduced in any form, stored in a retrieval system, or transmitted in any forms by any means - electronic, mechanical, photocopy, recording, or otherwise written.

without written permission of the author, PASTOR RASHAWN BEY except as provided by United States of America copyright law.

Unless otherwise, noted all Scripture quotations are from the King James Version (KJV) used by permission of public domain.

COPYRIGHT © 2023 BY PASTOR RASHAWN BEY

ALL RIGHTS RESERVED.

Dedication

I dedicate this book to my Lord and Savior, Jesus Christ, for being by my side and shaping me into the person I am today. He has given me the vision to write this book and inspire entrepreneurs, people of different backgrounds, those seeking a second chance, or a mentor. I dedicate this book to all of you.

Secondly, I want to dedicate this book to my lovely mother, Sheila Herrin. She gave birth to me and allowed me to exist in this world. Her tough love and honest conversations molded me, giving me the strength to face the struggles of life.

I also dedicate this book to my father, Joseph Ford. Many of my habits and traits come from him, and his spirit of exploration and willingness to try new things inspired me to write this book.

Next, I want to express my gratitude to my best friend, Calvin Ramsey. He was there for me during my lowest points, when I felt like there was no turning back. I am thankful to Pastor Ramsey for giving me a chance in ministry and allowing me to learn from my mistakes.

I dedicate this book to my children, Paris and Noah Bey. The love and support you show me every day inspire me to keep fighting and providing for our family. I hope this book becomes a part of our family legacy.

Lastly, I want to acknowledge my wife, Wanda Bey, for standing by my side during the tough times and helping me overcome struggles.

Together, we have proven that if we can endure hardships, we can overcome them.

To all those mentioned above, I dedicate this book with heartfelt appreciation and gratitude.

Table of Contents

Chapter 1: From Struggle to Success 1

Chapter 2: Why People Fail in Business 18

Chapter 3: Recreating Yourself 23

Chapter 4: So, You Think You're Not A Salesperson? 30

Chapter 5: Social Media Presence 46

Chapter 6: A lot can happen in 30 days 55

Chapter 7: It Takes Culture to Build an Empire 63

Chapter 8: Treat it like a Business! 69

Chapter 9: Tracking your data 76

Chapter 10: Powerful Online Tools 85

Chapter 11: Credit is Power 94

Chapter 12: Establish Your "Why?" 101

Chapter 13: Faith-Based Business with Profit 108

Chapter 14: Habits to Break 113

Chapter 15: Will Power over Skill 119

Chapter 16: Five Questions Gets All the Answers 125

Chapter 17: Work on Your Next 132

Chapter 18: Never Forget what it's like making $8hr 138

Chapter 19: Don't Forget to Give Honor 143

Daily Affirmation 149

Chapter 1

From Struggle to Success

Growing up in Oakland, California, statistics say I wasn't supposed to make it. Oakland was declared the murder capital of America. I was a C-average student and dropped out of college. I had terrible handwriting throughout elementary and junior high school. I was made fun of and picked on, and I had acne all over my face. I was always the last at everything and never played sports or won anything. When I did apply for sports, I wasn't picked for the team.

I grew up with my grandmother as a child, and it was a very sheltered upbringing. She kept me in the house all the time and was very strict. She raised me from a little boy until my teens.

My first year of high school was devastating, my grandmother passed away, and that was the beginning of my growing up. I moved in with my mother in my freshman year of high school, and that's when the transformation began.

I had to unlearn everything that I was taught growing up and I was forced to learn how to be a man and get a real job. My mother told me that I couldn't sit around and not work, so she searched for me a job working for the state of California.

I had no idea how to do an interview or anything else. I was going to show up for the interview with baggy jeans, Nike shoes, and a big T-shirt. My mom asked me what I was doing. She then dressed me up in a suit and tie and went over how to do an interview and answer the questions correctly.

The next day, I went to the interview and nailed it. I became the youngest person to work in that position for the state at the time. I was only 15 years old, and that's where my professionalism began.

When I started the job, I didn't know where to start and I was scared to death. That's when I ran into Aaron Ortiz, who changed my life with one piece of advice. He said, *"Whatever you do, wherever you go in your job, in business, and in life, learn everything beyond your title. Master your skills and become a valuable resource. By doing so, you'll always be in demand and have job security."*

That advice stuck with me till this day, at 38 years old. From that point on, I mastered everything in the company, and I started my journey in entrepreneurship. That's when I started my first MLM called, Vision One, which was an Internet company selling Internet service on a CD. Unfortunately, it didn't work, and everyone said it was a scam, which, to be honest, it really was.

I failed in that business and never made a dime, but I learned the most valuable lesson: the art of prospecting. I learned how to talk to anyone and everybody, regardless of age, nationality, or background. I had no fear, and that's how I utilize my strengths today.

After graduating from high school, I began to immerse myself in the street life, hanging out with the wrong crowd and indulging in various vices such as clubbing, drinking, smoking, and pursuing women. I kept moving back and forth between my mom's house and my friends' houses, thinking that the grass was greener on the other side.

However, I soon realized that I wasn't contributing anything and that my mom and others had grown tired of me. It finally dawned on me that home was the best place to be, a typical realization for a young person who thinks they know everything.

During this time, I ventured into another phase of entrepreneurship by selling CDs and bootleg movies. I transformed an illegal hustle into a more professional one. I stepped up my game, acquiring the necessary equipment and creating professional covers.

I always kept in mind the advice from Aaron Ortiz: learn everything, be a resource, and dominate. So, I made sure I outshined my competition, delivering better quality products and outperforming them in prospecting and follow-ups.

At some point, we decided to leave California, right before the economy took a turn for the worse. In 2004, we moved to Florida. I was incredibly excited, envisioning Miami or Orlando with palm trees, rollerblades, and beaches. However, upon arriving, I realized we were in Pensacola. I couldn't even pronounce it at first and jokingly thought it was "Pepsi-Cola."

It had a country vibe, and I hated it. I complained and said I wouldn't move there, but my mom insisted I give it another chance. She offered to pay for my flight if I came back and checked it out. So, I returned, got to know the people, and experienced the hospitality and food, plus I saw the untapped potential for my bootleg DVD business since nobody else was doing it. I decided to stay, and we settled in Florida.

From that point on, I networked and established a substantial clientele in a short period. At 19 years old, I was making an average of $3,000 to $4,000 per month. I was feeling on top of the world without any mortgage or even a cell phone bill.

Then one day, instead of going to the flea market as usual, I decided to hang out with a friend at the club. The next day, I woke up to a flurry of missed calls. A friend informed me that the feds raided the flea market and shut down all the DVD sellers.

At that point, I realized it was time to get out of that business. I closed everything down and started looking for new opportunities. That's when I stumbled upon the clothing business, specializing in tennis shoes, Jordans, Nikes, jeans, and more.

Once again, none of it was authentic. I turned another illegal hustle into a professional one. It's ironic how my mindset hadn't changed. However, I took it to a whole new level, becoming a big wholesaler, importing items from overseas, setting up stores, and generating a monthly income of $7,000.

With no bills to pay and no cell phone bill, I was living a life where everything I wore was for sale, directly off my own feet. I truly became a skilled salesman. I realized in my life that being successful can only last for so long when you're not doing the right thing. I ventured into drop shipping and ordering items for people, but many shipments were delayed or didn't arrive.

The accountability was lacking with the overseas suppliers who only accepted Western Union payments and didn't allow credit cards. I often found myself refunding customers. It was a business with no way to seek help from the police or take legal action. Eventually, this type of business became unsustainable.

However, I was determined to do whatever it took to find success again. One day, after Hurricane Katrina, I was at the mall where they sold shoes and urban gear. I noticed a guy buying multiple pairs of shoes, the same ones I had for sale but at full price. It struck me that he could buy them from me for a lower price. That's when I approached him and said, *"Hey, man, I have the same shoes in my car, and I can save you some money."*

He showed interest and I asked him for his name, he introduced himself as Quincy, but everyone calls him Q. I told him I would be right back, got his number, and went to the car. However, when I returned, he had vanished. I tried calling him repeatedly, but he didn't answer. I thought it was a crazy situation but shrugged it off.

Two months later, I received a call from him. He introduced himself as "Q" and explained that his phone had been dead, preventing him from returning my previous calls. He expressed interest in coming out to meet me and explore the possibility of doing business together, specifically selling shoes wholesale. I confirmed that I did offer wholesale options, so we set up a meeting with his partners. We discussed business, made plans, and started ordering shoes. That's when the next phase of my journey began.

As the shoes arrived, I got to know everyone involved, and we became friends. We started hanging out and even ventured into music together. I had my first experience as part of a gospel band, performing in musicals, and attending church more frequently. Even if I wasn't fully engaged in everything at the time, at least I was present and participating.

As time went by, my mom grew tired of living in Pensacola. She decided to move to Texas, and I agreed to go with her. We packed up everything, loaded it onto a U-Haul, and she left. I was supposed to drive and bring the dog, but something in my spirit told me that I couldn't keep following in my mom's shadow. I needed to transition from being a child to becoming a man and standing on my own two feet. It was a decision that seemed like the worst I could have made in my life.

I called my mom and told her that I was staying behind. She was furious, and I had to make a tough choice. I decided to stay, and I sent the dog her way. All I had left was the clothes on my back, my car, and a little gas money.

I was now homeless. Some of you may say that was the stupidest decision I could have made. I realize that many things in my life were born out of foolish choices. Like a tree that needs pruning to grow, sometimes our lives must go through an ugly trimming. It may appear that we're dying, but after the proper pruning, we grow back stronger and more beautiful than ever before.

That's how my life was. It had to go through an ugly pruning. I ended up sleeping in my car during the summer, unable to afford to keep the car running. It was the worst experience ever, but then I remembered my friend, Q who lived in Mississippi. I thought he might give me a place to stay. Ironically, his family took me in, and I was grateful for their kindness.

I was in a state where I had no family, no support, no job, no money, and relying on people I had recently met within the past year. Talk about stepping out on faith. But I was determined. Determined to make something of myself. Determined to prove everyone wrong.

I set out to establish connections and contacts, using the same methods I had used in the past to meet people and build relationships. So once again, I was trying to keep things going but my businesses started to slow down. The income wasn't coming in as it should and that's when Q suggested that I get a job.

My first job was at Future Pipe, where we made pipes out of resin. It was the dirtiest job, and I constantly felt filthy. I worked there for a while, but I grew tired of being treated poorly by a certain individual. One day, I confronted him and ended up throwing all my clothes in the trash and walking out. I never looked back. I think I was making $10 an hour at the time.

After that, I looked for a job at the shipyard. I had no idea what the shipyard was or how to do the job, but I was determined. I researched the position, which was called a chipper or grinder. It involved grinding welds to clean them up and working with metal. I went for the interview, even though I didn't know how to do the job. I figured they would either tell me I didn't have the job or give me a chance. I didn't want to walk around regretting not trying.

I passed the interview and got the job. When I started, I asked someone already working there to show me what I needed to do so I could learn quickly and get the job done. I became a master at what I did, becoming the top guy in the company, and the rest, as they say, is history.

However, I wasn't satisfied with just working for someone else. I wanted the freedom to be my own boss. So, I got into the car business. I obtained my auction license and opened my own car dealership.

A doctor provided us with the funding to get started, and we hit the ground running. I quit my job and dove into selling cars full-time. We were doing well for ourselves initially, but without a business mindset, professionalism, and proper expense management, we ended up in trouble.

Our car lot was the most ghetto-looking place you could imagine. It was a house converted into a car dealership, and I even lived there. When customers walked in, it looked like a living room with a TV. If they needed to use the bathroom, they had to pass by my bedroom. People asked if someone lived there, but we played it off and made excuses.

It's a funny situation to look back on. We were doing a great job selling cars and had a booming business, but we didn't prepare for things going wrong. We only planned for everything to go right. We made the mistake of buying a bad car that ended up costing us more in repairs than we would have made from selling it. It was a waste of money, and we kept losing and losing because we didn't want our reputation to be tarnished.

In the South, word travels fast when your reputation is bad, and we lost our contracts and line of credit. We ran out of money, and I had no choice but to get a job, even though I hated it. I swore to myself that I would never get involved in the car business again.

But of course, life took its twists and turns, and I found myself back in the car business. My girlfriend at the time suggested that I sell cars again. I called my best friend Calvin and asked for his opinion. He said that selling cars for Ford in the South would be a good opportunity. So, I applied and went for it.

Once again, I landed the interview and got the job. However, my friendship with Q deteriorated because I decided to leave the car business and pursue better opportunities. At the time, the only car I had was the one we were selling, and they always wanted it on the car lot, so they took it. Which left me with nothing but my belongings on the ground.

It was a tough day, a day of reckoning that I'll never forget. But it made me stronger. I worked hard at the dealership and became a top salesman within my first three months. They even gave me a car to drive. I was determined to succeed.

During my time in the car business, I met Pastor Trehvis Foster, initially thinking he was just a Bible-thumping hypocrite. However, he turned out to be a great friend and mentor. He taught me many biblical principles and showed me the true meaning of faith beyond just attending church.

Over the course of a year or two on the job, he ministered to me, and I made a decision to give my life to the Lord. It was the best thing that ever happened to me. As a result, my success in the car business skyrocketed. I went from making $40,000 a year to earning over $170,000 a year in the car business.

However, even when things were going well, the enemy continued to trail me. My friend and pastor, Trehvis Foster, passed away a year after I gave my life to the Lord. I was devastated and wondered where I would go to church and what I would do in ministry. That's when Pastor Willie Clark stepped in and declared that I was a preacher.

I was hesitant at first, but I embraced the call to ministry. I served under Pastor Willie Clark for a year and then joined Greater Texas Chapel with my spiritual father, Pastor Calvin Ramsey Senior, who was also the father of my best friend, Calvin Ramsey Junior. It was during this time that I learned a lot about myself, who I was becoming, and establishing my testimony.

After bouncing back from that storm and finding success in the car business, another storm hit. I went through a divorce, one of the most devastating moments in my life. It wasn't anyone's fault, but rather a result of getting married for the wrong reasons.

Sometimes people get married because they look good together or because it seems like the right thing to do, but they don't truly know each other or themselves. We were on different pages and eventually realized it. However, God blessed us with two beautiful children, Paris and Noah, who are the greatest gifts I could ever receive next to salvation.

After that chapter of my life, a new one opened when I met the woman who would become my wife, Wanda Farmer, now Wanda Bey. I had been in the car business for a while, and everything was going great until 2017 when the economy started to shift. Prices became too competitive, and the internet made it challenging to make a profit in the dealership. The dealership agreed to drop and transition to one-price selling. However, we didn't have much-used inventory, and my income dropped from $12,000 to $3,500 a month.

While $3,500 a month may not be bad for some, I had $7,000 in bills, including child support, mortgage, car notes, and ministry expenses. I couldn't even afford to continue working there because the money wasn't enough. I had to figure something out, and that's when the next chapter of my life began.

Mark Lee Jr. introduced me to Credit Repair, and we joined forces to create what we called, The Credit Solution Group. We made good money, and I had the courage to walk away from my job in 2018. I became an entrepreneur once again, enjoying the freedom of running my own business.

I set up an office and had a team, and everything seemed to be going great. However, after a year, everything fell apart because the people involved couldn't keep up with the skills necessary to be successful in the business. The multi-level marketing venture crashed, and now my bills are behind. My car and my wife's car were repossessed, and my mortgage is now $12,205 behind.

During that challenging period, my family and I struggled to make ends meet. I reached a point where my faith was tested, and I realized that my faith had been conditional. I relied on it only when things were going well for me. But God wanted me to truly rely on Him, even in the midst of difficulties.

It wasn't the material possessions or financial struggles that made me cry out to God; it was when my children asked me to spend time with them. They didn't understand that I was broke and behind on payments. All they wanted was to play with their dad. So, I promised them a trip to Chuck E. Cheese, but when I went to pay, my card was declined. I tried every card I had, but I had no money left. I had to face my screaming seven-year-old daughter and five-year-old son, who was confused as to why their dad didn't have $12.

It was a heartbreaking moment. On the drive home, my kids cried in the backseat, and I cried in the front, asking God why this was happening to me. I had always tried to do the right thing, not hurting anyone. I just wanted to be successful.

That night, I had a life-changing conversation with God. I made a vow to myself and to Him that I would never go through such a situation again. It was a powerful declaration, and I believed it with all my heart. It marked the end of all the struggles and failures because I stepped forward with unwavering faith and determination.

I received a call from my friend, Damian in California, who asked if I wanted to join him in the insurance business. I was initially hesitant because I was still focused on my credit repair business. However, Damian persisted and flew out to see me. After spending a few days together and seeing his income of $30,000 in a month, I decided to join him in the insurance industry with PHP, who was founded by our CEO Patrick Bet David and mentored under the Leadership of Matt And Sheena Sapaula.

This is when my journey in the insurance business began, and in my first year, I did over half a million dollars in business sales. Over the course of three and a half years, my team and I have generated over $4 million in business, acquired 3,500 customers, promoted 13 brokers, and currently have over 350 licensed agents and officers across the country.

All of this was achieved without a degree, despite going through a divorce, losing a child, experiencing credit issues, facing multiple repossessions, and even being homeless and encountering dangerous situations. Yet, God had a plan for my life, and I ended up successful.

Not only did I achieve success in the financial services and insurance industry, but I also became one of the most sought-after motivational speakers and Preachers in the country. I give all the glory, honor, and praise to God for His guidance and provision throughout my journey.

Notes

Notes

Chapter 2

Why People Fail in Business

You often hear stories of people failing in business, going out of business within the first year, or struggling to maintain overhead costs. However, the real reason why people fail in business is their attempt to avoid failure itself. It may sound contradictory, but when you try too hard to avoid failing, you end up failing anyway.

Failure is an integral part of the growth process. I want to emphasize that failing does not mean "Going out of business." You only truly fail when you give up and quit. To succeed, you must embrace failure and learn from it. It is through mistakes and setbacks that you gain valuable insights and improve.

No one is perfect, and mistakes are inevitable. Instead of fearing failure and making mistakes, confront them head-on. Expect to fail so that you can pave the way for success. If you don't plan to fail, you've already failed to plan.

Throughout my business journey, I have realized that every time I experienced a loss, it led to a significant comeback. There was a moment when all my brokers, the key players, income earners, and relationship builders, walked away simultaneously. It was a devastating blow, and I questioned what I did wrong. I thought I had done everything possible for them, provided support, and never betrayed their trust.

It was easy to blame them and believe it was entirely their fault. But then, one of my mentors, Tigran shared a powerful insight with me. He said, *"Everything sounds good when you blame others, but there comes a point where you have to look in the mirror and ask yourself, not what did you do wrong, but what could you have done better?"*

That hit me hard. I've always focused on what I hadn't done wrong and what others could have done differently, but I never took the time to reflect on how I could have improved during challenging times.

It's essential to find the areas where you can enhance yourself. Instead of dwelling on your accomplishments during good times, identify your leaks and constantly strive for improvement.

People tend to focus on the positives, but during good times, I always search for areas where I can become better. If you become too comfortable, you might find yourself blindsided by unexpected challenges.

Leaks are present every day, and you need to be vigilant. Ask yourself, "What could I have done to be better?" That was my teachable moment. Some of the most valuable life lessons come from losses, not victories. That particular loss grew my business by over 150%. It was the greatest comeback I could have experienced because I shifted my focus to what I could have done to be better.

I realized that building relationships was a key aspect I had neglected. Instead of solely focusing on business conversations, I should have invested more time in connecting with my team. I could have attended their birthday parties, bought them meaningful gifts, visited their churches, and organized retreats for us to travel together. If I had done all that, I am certain none of them would have quit.

By acknowledging my leaks, learning from my mistakes, and constantly seeking ways to improve, I ensured my success and avoided "Going out of business."

Notes

Notes

Chapter 3

Recreating Yourself

One of the most challenging experiences I've encountered in my life was the process of recreating myself. It proved to be a very difficult task as I embarked on a journey of not just changing who I am but enhancing the very best version of myself.

If you expect to achieve different results while continuing to engage in the same actions, you are simply deceiving yourself. You will never attain anything different by persisting in the same repetitive behavior; it is a form of insanity. You may find yourself striving for success at a higher level when, throughout your life, you have been accustomed to losing.

It becomes crucial to question why you haven't reached the desired destination or achieved the goals you aspire to. For instance, if you ponder why your credit score is below 700, a close examination of your habits is necessary.

If you consistently max out your credit cards and only pay off the balance at the end of each month, if you frequently make late payments or allow bills to accumulate, and if you never prioritize paying your bills promptly, you will never attain a credit score of 700.

Similarly, if you wonder why you haven't found a partner, it might be because your actions do not attract individuals who seek committed relationships. Perhaps the quality of your life is unappealing, and while your physical appearance may be attractive, your character traits fail to captivate others.

If you envision finding a perfect "10," yet you are realistically a "6" or even a "4," it is essential to recognize that you are not the person that matches the number you desire.

To make a change, you must first identify the aspects of yourself that need improvement or transformation. This necessitates a process of self-recreation.

To recreate oneself, seeking out examples of individuals who have already achieved what you aspire to become can be highly beneficial. Frequently, people make the mistake of seeking advice solely from those they like or relate to.

However, the information you need may not always come from individuals who are popular or aligned with your preferences. It is crucial to surround yourself with diverse perspectives and explore ideas and approaches that may initially feel uncomfortable or unfamiliar.

Just because you dislike something does not mean it lacks efficacy. Sometimes, you must go against your instincts and try an opposite approach. By doing so, you increase your chances of hitting the target you aim for. If what you have been doing has not yielded the desired results, it is evident that certain aspects of your behavior are holding you back.

To break free from this stagnation, you must upgrade your behavior, reinvent yourself, embrace novelty, display courage, conquer fear, and have unwavering faith. These attributes are essential for accomplishing something truly different.

Despite the initial challenges and discomfort that may arise, you must persist and remain consistent until you have completely recreated yourself, allowing your next best version to emerge.

A crucial aspect of this process is trust. Regardless of how unappealing or difficult things may appear at the beginning, you must trust the journey and commit to making the necessary changes.

Consistency is key. The next chapter of your life will not unfold if you are not willing to turn the page from where you are now. Only by leaving your current page behind can you recreate yourself and embark on a new chapter.

Reflecting on my own life, I underwent a phase of recreation, predominantly fueled by my faith during challenging moments. It was through these trials and tribulations that my faith grew stronger. I realized that I possessed far less faith than I initially believed, and it was in confronting adversity that I gained true conviction. I learned that tough times do not defeat you; instead, they fortify your strength.

With this realization, I began to challenge myself further. I made bold statements and declarations, speaking things into existence, even when I had no clue how they would materialize. I held onto the belief that anything is possible.

One scripture from the Bible that resonated with me is, *"With man, it may be impossible, but with God, all things are possible."* This became my guiding principle.

To recreate myself, I had to transform my thinking, shift my mindset, and, most importantly, change my heart. I had to reassess my values, reevaluate my perspectives, and alter my perception of the world. To see the path I was meant to follow, I had to discard the lens of my old way of thinking and adopt the perspective of a recreated person.

In conclusion, the process of recreating oneself commences with the mindset, beliefs, and faith. It requires embracing a new way of thinking, daring to do something different, and displaying boldness. If you commit to these actions, you will have no choice but to recreate yourself and embark on a transformative journey.

Notes

Notes

Chapter 4

So, You Think You're Not A Salesperson?

No, I don't like sales either.

I'm not good at sales.

I'm just not that type of person.

I don't want to be pushy.

I'm not good at convincing people.

You have all these excuses when it comes to the thought of being a salesperson, as if sales are a bad thing. Sales are the number one profession in the world when it comes to business. So, when you look at professions, the number one profession is financial services, followed by technology, healthcare, construction, real estate, education, food and restaurant, and entertainment.

The following businesses involves sales:
- » **Movies** are created so you can buy a ticket to watch them.
- » **Sports** are entertaining so you can go and watch them.
- » **Food** is made so you can pay to eat it.
- » **Real estate** is built so you can purchase it to live in it.
- » **Healthcare services** are provided so you can pay to utilize them.
- » **Financial services** are provided for you to pay and reap the benefits.

Everything revolves around sales. Yet, you still say,

I'm not a salesperson.

I don't have any experience convincing people.

That's why I work my job. I can come home and I don't have to convince anybody to do anything.

Well, I'm going to break your philosophy, change your perspective, and tell you that you are the best salesperson that you know. 'What? What do you mean?' Here's the reason:

- » The fact that you're convincing yourself that you're not a salesperson shows that you are. What do you mean? You just sold yourself on what you will never be, and you bought it. You bought a belief that you will never become a salesperson.

» Here's another example: if you're in a relationship, you sold your partner on why they should be with you. You presented yourself well-groomed, pampered, manicured, dressed nicely, and smelling good. You advertised yourself so your prospective partner could buy into being with you.

» Here's another example:

Have you ever planned a party?

Have you put a birthday party together?

Who did you tell?

You told everybody, right?

Let me change it. You advertised your event and you sold everybody on why they should come, right?

Here's a scenario:

You: *"Hey, what do you have going on this weekend?"*

Friend: *"I don't have anything going on."*

You: *"Oh, I have my birthday party this weekend. It's going to be awesome. There's going to be food, and there will be plenty of people and great music. You have to come out!"*

Friend: *"Well, I would, but I have anyone to watch my kids."*

You: *"No problem, bring your kids. Other people are bringing their kids too. There will be activities upstairs for them and you can relax downstairs."*

Friend: "Well, I would come, but I don't have anything to wear."

You: "Just come as you are. Don't worry about that, we're going to have a casual dress code."

Friend: *"Well, I would come, but I have to prepare for Sunday."*

You: "Listen, I'm telling you, you do not want to miss this party! Is there any way you can finish up early so you can come out, if only for an hour? It's going to be amazing!

Friend: *"Sounds like fun, I'll be there!"*

What did you just do? You convinced your friend why he/she should come to your party. You presented the benefits, advertised what's going to happen, and most importantly, you overcame every excuse or objection they had. This is a perfect description of a salesperson.

YOU ARE A SALESPERSON!

You have been selling all your life. Whether you were a kid trying to convince your parents to buy you something in the store, or you're a spouse trying to convince your partner to do something they didn't want to do.

Yes, you have been selling all your life, from telling people about a nice restaurant you went to, which is marketing.

MARKETING

Marketing is a key factor in sales. Marketing is when you tell others about something - why it was a great experience and why they should go there too. Here's what's amazing, you've been convincing people to do things and you've been doing it for free.

» You've been convincing people to support other businesses without a referral.

» You're the reason why movie theaters sell so many tickets because you tell people how great the movie was, and it makes them want to go and watch it.

» You convince people to try different restaurants because of your experience, which ultimately made those restaurants number one in the community.

SELLING

Selling is simply telling others about your experience and why they should follow your lead. Selling is not convincing; it's simply just telling. If you tell it well enough, they'll be convinced. Look at you, reading this and saying, *"Wow, I didn't even realize that I was a salesperson."*

Yes, you've been a salesperson! Even when you tell someone not to go somewhere, you're selling them on why they should make the opposite decision. Most importantly, you sell yourself every day on why you should get up early in the morning, why you should eat over here, why you should walk away from this, and why you haven't been doing this good.

WORDS ARE POWERFUL!

"Death and life are in the power of the tongue." Proverbs 18:21

You must be careful with your words because your words are powerful. If you do it long enough, you'll start to believe it. So, if you keep telling yourself what you're not, you're just convincing and selling yourself that you'll never be something. And if you keep speaking what you can't or won't do, it comes true. That's why it's so important to talk about what you're going to do, what you can become, who you are, and what you stand for.

Affirmations are the most powerful selling tools for you to convince yourself to be something extraordinary, excellent, great, and the best there ever was!

Here's an example of how there's power in what you say when it comes to selling: I was dealing with my editor of this book, Tammy Jae Swafford, and before asking her to help me with this book, I had known her for almost 10 years.

For 10 years, she always told me how busy she was working on her books and helping others with their books. She never once asked me if I knew anybody looking for a book to get published. I had never seen any of the books she has published, nor have I read any of the books she's published. But what's amazing about this scenario, is that we were partners in another business, and all I remember is that she always had a reason to not have time to work in our business.

She was always swamped and busy helping people with their books. Every other month I would talk to her, and she would say, *"I couldn't come to the meeting because I was finishing up with a client's book."*

"I've just been so stressed out."

"I'm working on a couple of books, trying to get these finished."

"We've been working on it for months now, we're almost finished."

"I need to take a break because I've been so busy."

All she did was work on these books, but when I thought about it, I said, *"Wow, her reputation with me was that she's always busy working on books."*

Fast forward 10 years, she's in another business with me, and she's still saying the same exact stuff. So, guess what happens later in my career? I decide to write a book and guess who pops up in my mind when I started to look up companies that can help me finish the book? Tammy. Out of all the editors and companies, she was the one that I trusted and felt the most comfortable with.

Now watch this: I had known about these other companies for a long time, I had seen their work, but I had never seen Tammy's work. I had never read any of her books or even seen what the finished product looked like. But why is it that I had so much trust in Tammy?

1. I personally know Tammy and the character that she has.

2. Knowing that we have been friends, I knew she would have my best interests from a friendship level.

3. The fact that she kept advertising her business subliminally by talking about how busy she was all the time.

Tammy talked about how publishing took up all her time, and even though they were complaints and excuses to me, they ended up being the strongest form of advertisement that I thought anybody could do. Because in my mind, if you've been doing books for over 10, 15, or 20 years, and it's taking up all your time.

You've been prioritizing it over everything. You've been stressed out about it, and you're currently working with different clients all the time. This told me that she had to be successful in doing it.

I had never seen one dollar she made. I had never seen a book. But common sense told me that if this is taking up all **her** time for 10 years and **she's** never worked a job, **she has** got to be making some money. So, I was sold.

This is the reason why I trusted her. It wasn't because she told me how good she was or how she could lay everything out. In fact, she never told me anything, yet I was sold on how busy she was.

As a salesperson, the best advertisement you can give yourself is when the prospect sees how busy you are, how dedicated you are, and how many people you're helping on a regular basis. That is proof within itself that you're successful because nobody can sustain working on something for 10 to 15 years without having some revenue coming in.

I shared this story with you to let you know that it's not about what you say, but it's all about how you are perceived by other people. So be careful what you complain about or say to people because you might be selling a nightmare.

"Oh man, times are rough, and I can't find anybody."

"Man, I haven't made any money yet."

"I haven't closed a sale in a long time."

"I haven't done this; I haven't done that."

"This customer backed out on me."

When you talk about these things to people, don't be surprised about why they're not supporting you. Clients/customers truly want to do business with people who are winning.

Think about it: if you're looking to sue somebody and you want to win the case, are you going to hire an inexpensive lawyer who will work with you, but is always losing and doesn't have any cases? No, because they're going to make you lose too. So, you don't look at the price, you look at the best. You're going to pay for the best because you know the best is going to help you win the big reward. So, be careful how you portray yourself to other people. Always present yourself as a winner and allow your actions to follow.

FOLLOW-UP

There's a fortune in the follow-up. Not everybody is going to say, "Yes!" or close the deal the first time you present it. Did you know that the biggest sales deals happen behind closed doors? The most important sale you'll probably ever run into is the one that is birthed out of the follow-up.

Many people don't follow up. They're afraid of being that person who bugs, chases, or hounds others. But it's all about perspective. If you see yourself as a person who has a solution, who has the answer to their problem, then you become more confident when it comes to bringing up certain topics. Because you realize that you're not trying to sell to them, you're serving their needs and you're helping them.

So, one of the biggest problems I see, is that people talk to prospects and after that day, nobody calls, nobody checks on the person, and nobody follows up. They just expect the person to automatically be all in. They expect people to not have any questions. They expect a perfect world when in reality, it doesn't work that way. You have to remind a person why doing business with you would be beneficial to them.

To be honest with you, I'm a product of the follow-up in my current field in the financial industry. I was followed up with five times before I said, *"Yes."* Believe it or not, I said no five times, and I always think back and say, *"What if they would've stopped at the fifth no? Where would I be today?"* I thank God every day that they followed up with me on the sixth follow-up, and I came into the business.

So, when it comes to follow-up, there are some key things you need to know. Follow-up isn't always about asking the person,

"What did you think about it?"

"Do you want to get started?"

"Do you want to buy the car before it's too late?"

Those questions are more about tactics.

Follow-ups are about just checking on the person, seeing how everything is going, and asking if they have any questions. When you ask those questions, you put them in a position to drop their guard down because they believe you're going to ask a concerned question vs a tactic question. By nature, they can say, "Yeah, I want to talk about this." Those words are an alert to you that you have what they're looking for. Remember, a person will always tell you how they want to be sold. So, ask questions to figure out what's important to them.

Following up can also involve bringing their awareness to something they may have missed, like an article, an event, or a current situation. It distracts them from thinking about the initial reason for your call and gets them to focus on the new situation. Then you can follow up and ask if they have looked at everything. That's one of the best ways to follow up.

Keep in mind, there's a sequence of follow-ups.

» Typically, you want to follow up 4 to 5 hours later, unless it's already nighttime. Call the person, text, or email and say, "I just want to thank you for taking time out with me today because I know you didn't have to. I just wanted to express my gratitude." Let them talk, as your gratitude changes their attitude.

Most people don't thank others for just taking time out of their day. They think that people are entitled to spend time with them. So, when you thank someone, their guard drops, and they become more open to answering your next phone call. This is when you can ask if they have any questions and if they haven't already scheduled an appointment, ask them for a good day to get together and go over the details.

- » Remember, the faster you follow up for the appointment, the more successful you'll be. If I don't talk to a person within 4-5 hrs., I'll talk to them the next day, but no less than 24 hours.

- » You want to follow up so that you can book your next appointment. But the key is: not to talk too much about what you've already discussed but ask if they have any questions and thank them for taking time out of their day.

- » The next follow-up is after seven days if there's no appointment booked, then 21 days, and then the 30-day mark, two-month mark, six-month mark, and 12-month mark.

- » Some of my best business partners and clients today are people who I followed up with for over a year. I made sure I put them in positions where they could see me constantly.

- » Do you want to the know the best secret when it comes to following up? No, it's not calling or checking on them, but it's actually adding them to your social media page.

Every day they have no choice but to see what you're doing. Every day they see your product, your success stories, and everything you do on your social media feed. A visual view of you helping others makes them more likely to come on board.

There's a fortune in the follow-up!

In conclusion, when you think you're not a salesperson, you really are. You're either selling an event, a service, a product, an appointment, the philosophy, the relationship, and even yourself. Remember, everything is sales. If you use the keys given in this chapter, you'll master the skill.

You can't lose but is proven to win!

Notes

Notes

Chapter 5

Social Media Presence

Social media is the way of the present and will continue to be the future. I remember when the closest thing to social media was browsing ads in the newspaper or placing ads for dating or making connections.

Then came Craigslist, and after that, the party line where you could call a number and join rooms to meet new people. If you didn't like one room, you could switch to the next. It was exciting, although the phone bills were expensive.

Later, Myspace became popular, allowing users to create customizable profiles with graphics, music, and more. It was a platform where you could express yourself.

As time passed, social media platforms evolved, including Black Planet, Yahoo! Messenger, and eventually, Facebook, Instagram, TikTok, and YouTube, which completely changed the game. Social media has generated millions for my business and helped me establish relationships.

Facebook has been my primary platform, where I have promoted my clothing sales, sold cars, advertised my credit repair business, ran my ministry, and currently run my financial and life insurance firm.

While there were traditional prospecting methods such as knocking on doors, distributing flyers, and using mailers or telemarketing, those approaches are outdated and time-consuming.

I want to share how I made millions on social media in my career working for a car dealership and in my own business. When it comes to social media, building relationships is key. You can't solely rely on your business profile, especially if you're just starting out and people don't know your brand. People do business with those they like and trust.

Simply having a business page won't automatically drive traffic unless you offer something unique and in demand. The secret to building my business on social media was leveraging my personal page.

As the songwriter Jay-Z said, *"I'm not just a businessman; I'm a business man."*

It's true; you are the brand and the business. Merge your personal and business identities. You don't have to wear two hats or pretend to be someone you're not. Be consistent with who you are because true consistency can only come from being yourself.

I embraced these principles and found a way to merge my personal identity with my business. It was a genius move because I didn't have to pretend or change who I was. I remained true to myself every day.

To start building a social media presence:

1. It's important to have a professional picture. You don't need an expensive photoshoot; a well-taken photo with an up-to-date smartphone will do.

2. Dress nicely, find an area with natural light (avoid direct sunlight), and take a clear picture using portrait mode against a solid wall or background.

3. You can then crop the picture and place yourself against a solid white background using photo editing apps.

4. Upload this image to your profile, and it will give you a professional headshot that looks impressive on social media.

People want to do business with those who appear successful, regardless of the industry. I recently spoke with one of my coaches, Matt Sapaula, who shared an interesting story.

A professional athlete asked him how much he was making, and when Matt told him his income, the athlete said, *"I want you to help me with my money."* The athlete's perspective was that if Matt wasn't making a similar income to his income, how could he help him?

People often judge based on appearances, so looking successful and carrying yourself as a winner will attract others who are already successful. First impressions matter, and you can't have a second chance to make a first impression.

Keep this in mind as you update your profile picture and bio.

1. Your profile picture should align with your brand, and your bio is an opportunity to introduce yourself.

2. Declare who you are, whether it's an entrepreneur, a mom, an athlete, a motivational speaker, or an author.

3. People read bios, so make it interesting and relevant.

4. Another crucial aspect is the content you post on your page. Avoid low-quality pictures of partying, alcohol, weed, or working on cars in a dusty environment. Everything you post should reflect quality and align with your brand.

For example:

- » If you're selling jewelry, post pictures that showcase your everyday activities.

- » If you have a picture of your kids, capture the best moment with them. If they take their first steps, record it with high quality.

- » Show your family doing something enjoyable that resonates with your target audience's aspirations.

Consistency is vital in social media. To effectively manage your schedule, understand the best time frames when people are most active on social media. Also, familiarize yourself with the algorithm, which determines the visibility of your content.

Facebook uses algorithms to put users in front of more people based on their activity. By analyzing engagement, Facebook can pitch advertisements to businesses.

To build your following organically, search for the right people to connect with. Look for individuals who align with your business goals, such as:

- » Married couples
- » Homeowners
- » Parents
- » Entrepreneurs
- » Community leaders.

Add them as friends, engage with their posts, and send messages to initiate conversations. However, be cautious not to overdo it to avoid being penalized by Facebook.

By consistently engaging with the right market, you'll start building your influence, social media presence, and trust. The goal is to reach a point where you have a larger number of organic followers.

» When posting content, aim for engagement by creating posts that resonate with everyone. For example, a simple post like "If God has been good to you, shout 'Amen!'" can generate many comments and engagement.

» Ask people to comment, like their comments, and reply with positive responses. This boosts Facebook's algorithm, ensuring your posts reach a wider audience. Strive for a good ratio between likes, comments, and shares.

Ideally, if you have 50 shares, you should have 200 comments and 400 likes. These numbers indicate that you're building influence and attracting engagement.

Once you've established your influence and trust, you can confidently promote your business to your followers. When you share posts about your business, your existing followers are more likely to engage with them. This is how you build your social media presence effectively.

Remember, social media is a powerful tool that, when utilized correctly, can lead to tremendous success in business. Building your presence takes time and effort, but by following these steps and maintaining consistency, you will gradually attract the right clients or customers, establish trust, and achieve your business goals.

Notes

Notes

Chapter 6

A Lot Can Happen in 30 Days

Absolutely right, a lot can happen in 30 days, to be honest with you. A lot can happen in 30 minutes, but I want to talk about how much can happen in 30 days. I've lived in multiple states, and I've been the person who had to start all over again, making new friends, meeting new people, establishing new contacts, finding a new church home, and so on. I even forgot where all the stores were.

However, I realized that it was surprisingly easy to go from having nothing to becoming what you could call the "mayor" of the town in just 30 days. You can go from not knowing a soul to becoming the most popular person in the community.

So, let me share with you how I was able to move to Florida, Mississippi, and Texas and build relationships and a network as if I had lived there my whole life.

The first step:

» Get on social media and start adding people who live in the city where you're trying to build connections. But not just anybody, the number one person you want to find is the pastors because they already have an established presence in the community. So, getting to know them and connecting with the people in their churches is crucial.

» Additionally, it's important to get to know all the realtors in the area since they have sold most of the houses to the people living in the community.

» Also, seek out teachers, restaurant owners, and other business owners in the area.

Next:

» Go to every mall in the city and get to know the people who work there. They will be there every day and have interactions with people. You can connect with people working in cell phone booths, jewelry stores, shoe departments, and department stores where they sell perfume, among other areas.

» Engage with them, mentioning that you're new to the area and looking to meet new people. Ask for restaurant recommendations or suggestions for places to go.

» Find out where the local Chamber of Commerce is located. It's another place where you can establish connections, meet influential individuals, and get referrals and recommendations.

» Additionally, explore the biggest flea market in the area. This is where all the people and business owners gather, providing you with opportunities to network and even get a booth to display your products.

» Visit churches in the community and, if you're bold, stand up when they ask if there are any visitors. Introduce yourself, mentioning that you've recently moved to the area and opened a new business offering financial services or whatever your business is about.

» Express your excitement about being there, enjoying the service, and looking forward to getting to know the ministry and everyone in the congregation.

» See, you just advertised your business in less than 60 sec. without trying to sell anything. Make eye contact with people at the end of the service, shake their hands, and exchange contact information. Offer them your business card, introduce yourself further, and express interest in connecting with them.

» Try to have lunch with pastors, organization leaders, mayors, congressmen, and other city officials. You can even offer to take them out to lunch and make a small donation to their campaigns. This can go a long way as doing business with people often leads to them doing business with you.

» When it comes to restaurants, find one that has a lot of people and make it your regular spot. Have a routine where you sit in the same seat, interact with the staff, and build relationships. Soon, they will recognize you, welcome you back and know your preferences. Engage with everybody working there, and conversations about professions or businesses will naturally arise. This helps you establish connections and get into the market. You may even start receiving invitations to parties and events.

» Coffee shops are where entrepreneurs often gather, so strike up conversations with people working on their laptops or engaging in discussions. Eavesdrop on their conversations to find connections and inquire about what they do for a living. This can lead to interesting conversations and opportunities.

» Look for events where you can become a vendor to showcase your products or services. This could include book author events, real estate expos, first-time homebuyer workshops, and any other event where you can get a vendor opportunity.

» Attend outdoor events, festivals, and carnivals where you can be seen by a large audience.

» Visit local businesses such as cleaners, financial places, restaurants, and gas stations. Every business usually has a spot where you can leave your business card. Make sure your business card includes your picture and leave 5-6 cards at each business with a designated business card section. By doing this consistently, people will start recognizing your face and getting to know you wherever they go.

» Collect as many business cards as you can from local businesses and contact them to learn more about what they do. This allows you to establish connections and get to know them better.

- » Don't overlook places like car detail shops and locations where parents gather to watch their kids play in local games. Coaches, in particular, know a lot of people since they've coached many children. These can be valuable connections.

- » Lastly, Walmart is one of the easiest places to prospect. You can walk around Walmart and run into different people each time. Nobody will bother you if you approach people and hand out your business card to those who are shopping. Walmart attracts a constant flow of people, providing ample opportunities to meet and get to know individuals in the community.

If you follow these strategies, I promise you will become the "mayor" of your community and build your business within 30 days. You will get to know everybody in a short time.

Remember, it only takes one person to create an explosion in your business. By meeting one person who leads you to another, and then another, you can land a big deal and accomplish more in 30 days than you might have in an entire year. **A lot can happen in 30 days!**

Notes

Notes

Chapter 7

It Takes Culture to Build an Empire

I used to think that I knew how to build a company because of my experiences as a manager or supervisor at my job. I even hired family members to work with me in the business. However, being a manager or supervisor does not automatically make you qualified to be a successful business owner. There's a difference between being self-employed and being a business owner.

When you're self-employed, all your efforts are dependent on you. For example, if you're a real estate agent, a snowball stand owner, a plumber, a lawyer, or a doctor, your income is directly tied to your personal efforts. If you don't work, you don't make any money.

On the other hand, a business owner has systems and processes in place that generate income whether they are personally working or not. It took me some time to realize this distinction. I thought being self-employed and being a business owner were the same, but I came to understand that I was just self-employed.

So, what are the key things to consider when it comes to running a business?

1. One important aspect is having people working with you. Their efforts contribute to generating passive income, independent income, and exponential growth. It's important to recognize that a thousand people working together will always outperform a solo entrepreneur.

2. If you break down the hours, as a solo entrepreneur, you have eight hours a day to work. However, if you have ten people working with you, each working eight hours, that's a total of 80 hours of work. This demonstrates the power of duplication. The question then becomes: how do you get people to work independently and contribute to the growth of the business?

3. When dealing with a team of volunteers or 1099 contractors, as opposed to being a manager or supervisor, you can't force them to work for you. They have the

option to work elsewhere if a better opportunity comes along.

4. As a business owner your role is to provide leadership. You must create a culture that motivates and inspires them to stay and be part of the team. Culture is the biggest asset in a business because it fosters loyalty and commitment.

5. To build a successful business with a team, you need to create a culture and environment where people have fun and enjoy their work. This could include recognition, traditions, status, team-building activities, or any other elements that establish a positive and motivating culture. Culture creates a sense of belonging and long-term commitment.

In our company, we prioritize culture by mirroring the dynamics and competitiveness found in professional sports. We interact with people and create an energetic and structured environment. After all, what people remember and value the most is how they were treated, recognized, and the overall experience they had.

Our company incorporates various formats like March Madness championships, World Class Travel, Bonuses, Kilos of Gold, team chants, Ladies' retreats, and women empowerment, which instill a sense of fun and excitement. A strong culture is evident when no amount of money can tempt someone to leave because they feel connected and committed.

Consider incorporating culture-building activities into your business, such as praying together as a team, going out to eat, or any other activities that foster a sense of community and excitement. When you have a strong culture, it will drive and motivate everyone to stay committed, regardless of financial offers.

Notes

Notes

Chapter 8

Treat it like a Business!

This statement holds a great deal of truth. It's not uncommon for individuals to wonder why they're not getting paid or why they haven't seen significant results despite being in the same state for a while.

The underlying reason often lies in the fact that they haven't treated their business as a legitimate enterprise; instead, they've approached it more like a casual hobby. We have a saying, *Treat it like a hobby it will pay you like a hobby, but if you treat it like a business, it will pay you like a business.* This distinction is a critical element of entrepreneurship, as it requires a deep respect for the business and a commitment to treating it as such.

When it comes to being an entrepreneur, one must set their schedule and conduct themselves as if they are working for their own company.

This means:

» Adhering to a consistent routine.

» Avoiding late starts and irregular sleep patterns that can quickly wear down both the body and the business.

» Moreover, it entails establishing a distinct business name and developing a recognizable brand.

Even if one is unable to create a brand on the scale of a large corporation, having a personal brand outside of it is still crucial.

This personal brand represents a sense of ownership, both in the present and as a future legacy to be passed on to family members or successors. It becomes something tangible, motivating the entrepreneur to take their business more seriously.

In order to mentally position oneself as a business owner, there are several practical steps that can be taken:

1. First, visit **irs.gov** and obtain an **Employer Identification Number (EIN)** for the business, under its name allows for the opening of a dedicated business bank account.

2. Additionally, register the business as a **Limited Liability Company (LLC)** with the Secretary of State or

Department of Revenue in the respective state. An LLC provides a legal foundation for your business.

3. Professional photographs featuring the entrepreneur's image alongside the business name can be taken and utilized on business cards, further reinforcing the brand.

4. Designing logos helps to establish a consistent visual identity, contributing to effective branding efforts.

5. Creating a dedicated business Facebook page and ordering checks through the business bank account are additional measures that add professionalism and credibility to the enterprise.

By undertaking these necessary steps, entrepreneurs can begin to take their businesses more seriously. It's often challenging to treat it with the same level of dedication when there haven't been significant investments made.

However, as an entrepreneur starts building their brand and reinvesting in their business, a stronger connection and sense of ownership over the enterprise naturally develops. It no longer feels like simply working for the business; instead, it becomes an extension of oneself and the values they hold.

This shift establishes a system and flow within the organization, enabling the entrepreneur to fully embrace their role as a business owner.

It's important to recognize that taking ownership of a home business is essential. When asked about their occupation, many entrepreneurs find that their family members are unaware of the nature of their work.

This lack of awareness often stems from a failure to run the business in a manner that commands respect and professionalism. By treating the business seriously, other family members will be more likely to support and understand its significance. It's crucial to strive towards treating the business as a true enterprise, as this shift in perspective will ultimately garner more support and recognition from loved ones.

In summary, acknowledging the distinction between treating a business as a hobby versus running it as a professional enterprise is key to achieving success as an entrepreneur.

By adopting a professional mindset, entrepreneurs can establish a structured routine, create a distinctive brand, and undertake practical steps such as obtaining an EIN, registering the business, and developing a consistent visual identity.

As the business takes on a more substantial presence, the entrepreneur will experience a deepened sense of ownership and commitment. Furthermore, by treating the business with the respect it deserves, family members and others will recognize its importance and offer their support.

Notes

Notes

Chapter 9

Tracking Your Data

Man, I was never a numbers person. I wasn't really a genius in school. I was a C student, and I only went up to algebra. But what I found valuable in business is the importance of tracking data. Data is the only information that tells you the truth. Men lie, women lie, people lie, but numbers don't lie.

I developed this philosophy because I got frustrated with the constant stress of trying to figure out if I was doing well or poorly in my business. I struggled to measure my success accurately. I used to rely on how I felt, but emotions can cloud judgment, especially when we want to feel like champions all the time.

Our feelings often dictate how we perceive the outcome of our day, whether it will be good or bad. When it's a bad day, you feel it, and it affects not only you but also your customers, team, significant other, and even your children. Everyone can sense when you're having a tough day in business. This plays a significant role in how we perform.

Mentors used to tell me that I was "winging" my business, meaning I was just throwing things against the wall and hoping they would stick. I didn't have a clear understanding of what I was doing or where I was going. I relied solely on talent and tried to accomplish as much as possible throughout the day, week, month, and year.

However, I lacked specific goals and a sense of direction. I didn't even know if I was on track. That's when I realized that the missing key component was data.

Data, in simple terms, refers to numbers that measure your performance. Once I learned how to track my data, everything became simpler and easier. I could predict whether I was on track, determine what we were going to achieve, and assess whether we were surpassing or falling short of our goals for the month, day, week, and year.

So, how do I measure? First and foremost, your greatest competition isn't other companies or top salespeople. Your biggest competition is yourself. You compete not only with the person you are today but also with the person you were yesterday.

That's where numbers come into play. When I measure numbers, I follow a formula. I compare where I am today with where I was at the same time last year. I dig into the precise details, looking at the exact day.

Some of you might not have a tracker to measure this, but I recommend starting today and tracking your daily activities. This data will provide you with insights into what you did on the same day last year.

For example, let's say that on May 6th last year, I only made a certain number of sales or had no sales at all. I then compare it to how many sales I have on that same day this year. My goal is to beat what I achieved on the 8th of last year compared to the 8th of this year. If I made two sales on the 8th of last year, I need to make at least two sales today to break even with last year.

If I make one more sale, I'm up, and if I make two more, I've doubled what I did last year, marking a 100% increase. This method allows me to assess my progress and determine how close I am to the numbers I achieved last year.

By comparing my performance over the first 4 1/2 months of this year to the same period last year, I can evaluate my progress. I measure how far I am from the numbers I achieved during the first 5 or 4 1/2 months of last year, as well as the first six months and the entire year of last year.

If I'm already at the same number as I achieved last year during this period, it indicates that I'm having a successful year. Even if I'm not performing at my best, I still congratulate myself because I'm surpassing last year's results.

This approach helps me track data and ensures that my biggest competitor is always myself. Having a good month isn't enough; if I don't beat last year's performance, I consider it a subpar year.

Another way to use data is by creating a tracker aligned with your projections. Let's say I want to achieve 100 sales this month. I divide it into four weeks and calculate the number of sales I need to make per day to reach that goal.

For instance, if I allocate 30 days to keep it simple, I divide the 100 sales by four weeks, which gives me 25 sales per week. Breaking down the weekly target, I aim for an average of six sales per day to maximize the week's performance. If I make five sales per day for five days a week, I will reach 100 sales for the month. This method allows me to measure my performance against my projected targets.

Measuring the closing ratio is another way of using data. It tells you the number of people you need to interact with to close a deal. For example, if you close one deal for every ten people you talk to, your closing ratio is 10%. By measuring this ratio, you can gauge the amount of activity required to achieve your desired results.

In our company, we follow a rule called the 10-3-1 rule, which states that for every ten people we invite, three will show interest, and one will actually get started. By measuring this, we can assess our closing ratio and adjust our activities accordingly. If we exceed one person getting started for every ten invites, our closing ratio improves.

Understanding that it's a numbers game, you increase your chances of success by talking to more people. Many times, people focus on talking to a few individuals and then do nothing for the rest of the day.

It's important to fill your day with activity because activity leads to results. Remember, it's not about celebrating the results; it's about celebrating the activity because activity eventually yields results.

Engage in activities that don't require much thought to maximize your productivity. Regardless of talent, skill, drive, or determination, consistent activity will yield numbers.

If you want to succeed, focus on the numbers, and talk to as many people as possible. By nature, engaging with more people increases your chances of closing deals. Implement a system with consistent scripts and tones to communicate the same message to as many people as you can. Eventually, you will encounter individuals who will get started, and you will come across three types of people: A-people, B-people, and C-people.

» **A-people** are those who join your business but don't do much. They are easily discouraged, slow starters, overthinkers, and noncoachable. They sporadically take action but won't achieve extraordinary results.

» **B-people** are more reliable. They do what you ask them to do, achieve decent numbers, and stick around. They may take longer to complete tasks but have the potential to become something more significant over time.

» **C-people** are the elite of the elite. They are 100% coachable, achieve record-breaking results, obtain licenses or certifications, show dedication in all aspects of life, and constantly aim for personal growth. C-people are your future brokers and leaders.

To measure all of this, rely on data. Study behavior, observe trends, and remember one principle: how a person does one thing is how they do everything. Notice patterns in people's actions and their consistency across various aspects of life. If someone is unreliable or lacks integrity in one area, chances are they will demonstrate the same behavior in other areas.

Character is tested during tough times, and tough times reveal true character. Therefore, use the data you gather to make informed decisions about who you want to do business with and who you should avoid.

In conclusion, data is a powerful driver in everything you do, from your business interactions to your personal relationships. It allows you to measure success, determine whether you're on the right track, and assess whether you're achieving your goals.

Remember to measure your performance against previous records and focus on beating your own best. Don't get comfortable with one-time achievements; strive to consistently surpass your prior accomplishments. Ultimately, data empowers you to make informed decisions and achieve long-term success.

Notes

Notes

Chapter 10

Powerful Online Tools

There are several tools you will need to run your business. If you try to wing it and rely solely on talent without proper organization, your business won't scale effectively. To organize yourself, you need to use specific tools. I'll provide you with several tools that I've used to grow my business empire successfully.

1. **Saving Money -** The first key to business success is saving as much money as possible. While you shouldn't be cheap, finding ways to save a dollar while getting the job done is crucial.

   I'll now share some tools that can save you money and time while allowing you to work on your own schedule. These tools also promote independence, eliminating the need to rely on developers or others to complete tasks.

2. **Google Docs** - One of the essential tools is Google Docs. It allows you to create and access PowerPoint presentations, documents, PDFs, and Excel spreadsheets. Setting up a Gmail account will give you complete and efficient access to Google Drive, which offers ample storage space.

   With Google Docs, you can work on your presentations anywhere, if you have internet access on your cell phone, tablet, computer, or laptop.

   Additionally, it provides live streaming capabilities, allowing you to play YouTube videos directly in your presentations. Google Drive enables easy sharing, granting access for others to view, download, and edit your files in real-time.

3. **Google Slides** - Another tool in the Google Drive suite is Google Slides, which is perfect for creating professional PowerPoint presentations. It offers the same advantages as Google Docs, with the added benefit of automatic saving and instant updates for anyone with access to the presentation. You can even make edits during a presentation, and the changes will be immediately visible to your audience.

4. **Google Drive** - For Word Processing needs use Google Drive which includes Google Docs. With this tool, you can type and edit documents on the go, eliminating the need for desktop software.

5. **Google Sheets -** Additionally, Google Sheets within Google Drive is excellent for creating customizable Excel spreadsheets to track your team's numbers, goals, and rankings. It allows you to organize data numerically or alphabetically, making it easier to monitor and motivate your team's progress.

6. **PosterMyWall -** If you need to design eye-catching flyers or banners for your business, I highly recommend using PosterMyWall.com. This site offers numerous templates that you can customize by changing pictures and text, allowing you to create professional designs quickly and easily.

   PosterMyWall covers various formats, dimensions, and layouts, ensuring your creations are suitable for social media, websites, or print.

7. **QuickBooks Online -** For accounting purposes without hiring a dedicated accountant, QuickBooks Online is an excellent tool. It allows you to link your bank accounts, categorize expenses, and generate profit and loss statements. QuickBooks Online simplifies financial management, providing you with accurate and up-to-date insights into your business's performance.

8. **Zoom -** In terms of communication tools, Zoom is a must-have. It enables face-to-face meetings, screen sharing, virtual

backgrounds, and recording capabilities. Zoom is versatile and convenient, allowing you to connect with clients, partners, and team members from anywhere in the world. Zoom is particularly useful for remote presentations, troubleshooting, and conducting online training sessions.

9. **Wix.com** - For website creations, Wix.com is highly recommended. It offers user-friendly templates and customization options, allowing you to build a professional website without extensive coding knowledge. Wix provides features like appointment booking and integrates well with various marketing tools. It's a cost-effective solution for establishing an online presence.

10. **YouTube** – YouTube is another valuable tool for business. It allows you to upload and store videos, making them accessible to your team or the public. You can set videos to unlisted or private if you only want specific individuals to access them. YouTube is an excellent platform for training, promotional videos, and increasing your online visibility.

11. **Instagram & Facebook -** To enhance your social media presence, I recommend using Instagram to reach a younger audience and Facebook to connect with a more mature demographic. Instagram is ideal for visual content and building

a substantial following, while Facebook offers broader functionality, including event management and personal connections.

12. **DocuSign** - For document signing, DocuSign is a widely accepted and secure platform. It allows you to send documents electronically, track signatures, and maintain a verification trail. DocuSign ensures efficiency and legality in document processing, eliminating the need for physical paperwork.

13. **Cash App & Venmo** - To handle financial transactions, Cash App and Venmo are convenient options. They allow seamless money transfers and are widely accepted by individuals and businesses alike.

14. **Reliable Internet Connection** - Having a reliable internet connection is crucial, especially when conducting business on the go. Ensure your cell phone has hotspot capability to serve as a backup internet source when needed.

15. **Clicker** - If you frequently deliver presentations, consider purchasing a clicker. It allows you to control your slides remotely, even if your computer is far away from the presentation area.

16. **QR codes** - To replace physical business cards, consider creating digital versions that can be easily shared via email or

messaging apps. QR codes can also be used for instant access to your contact information.

17. **Business Cards** - Here's another secret if you want to print cards to hand out and don't have time to wait a week for shipping. Go to Office Depot or Staples.com, email your design (or you can upload your design), and print 4 to a page on a 3x5 cover paper.

When you pick up your cards, ask the salesperson to cut your cards, now you have 4 cards, while only paying for 1 sheet. Now on the same day, you can have your marketing material for your event on demand.

18. **PDFfiller** - For fillable documents and forms, PDFfiller is an excellent tool. It enables you to create, edit, and save documents digitally, making information collection and organization more efficient.

19. **Laptop** - Lastly, it is advisable to invest in a lightweight laptop with long battery life. This ensures portability and productivity, enabling you to work efficiently even when you're on the move.

Remember to use your phone's calendar to:

- » Set reminders!
- » Schedule appointments!
- » Stay organized!

It's a convenient way to keep track of important dates, meetings, and payment reminders. Moreover, consider setting up reminders for clients to ensure they don't forget their monthly payments.

By utilizing these tools effectively, treating your business seriously, and maintaining efficient systems, you can achieve success and significantly grow your business without spending excessive amounts of money.

Notes

Notes

Chapter 11

Credit is Power

When it comes to venturing into business, one of the most significant mistakes I made was relying solely on my personal funds. I soon discovered the importance of OPM (Other People's Money) as a key principle in business.

The reason behind this is, when starting out with limited capital, every single dollar is crucial. Making decisions based on emotions and personal financial constraints rather than sound business judgment can hinder the growth and success of your venture.

Using your own money creates a sense of urgency to see an immediate return on investment. You find yourself under pressure to sell quickly or make desperate decisions just to cover expenses or pay bills.

This rush mindset prevents you from letting your investments develop and flourish naturally over time. It limits your ability to negotiate effectively or explore long-term opportunities. Instead, you're forced to focus on short-term gains, often sacrificing profitability in the process.

Understanding the power of credit changed my perspective entirely. Credit allows you to access funds that belong to others, providing you with the luxury of patience and the ability to wait for investments to mature and yield optimal results.

By utilizing credit wisely, you can separate your personal finances from your business activities, ensuring that you make decisions based on solid business principles rather than immediate financial constraints.

Here's a practical strategy to employ when leveraging credit in your business. Let's say you have a credit card with a $5,000 limit. In a given month, you can use the card to cover your business expenses, including advertising costs, bills, and other necessary expenditures.

As the following month begins, you have two options based on the profits generated:

> » Option one involves using the profits to pay off the credit card balance entirely. This approach allows you to eliminate any debt and maintain a clean financial slate.

» Option two comes into play if the following month proves slower, resulting in lower profits. In this case, you can pay the minimum amount due on the credit card while using the remaining funds to cover your bills and essential expenses.

This flexibility enables you to navigate through periods of lower income without draining your personal finances or resorting to high-interest loans.

By strategically managing your credit, you maintain a healthy cash flow and preserve your own funds for future opportunities, emergencies, or personal needs.

The next month, if you experience a significant inflow of revenue, you can pay off the credit card balance in full, effectively resetting the cycle. This approach allows you to reuse the credit card as needed, leveraging it to facilitate business operations without depleting your cash reserves.

However, it's essential to note that this credit strategy is most effective when you have a steady and reliable income stream in your business. Without a consistent flow of revenue, it can be challenging to manage credit obligations and meet financial commitments.

It's crucial to establish a solid foundation for your business, ensuring that you have a reliable income source before embarking on this credit-based approach.

In summary, by utilizing OPM (Other People's Money) in the form of credit, you can free yourself from the limitations and pressures of using your own funds. This strategy allows you to make sound business decisions, negotiate effectively, and patiently wait for investments to mature.

By using credit wisely and maintaining a healthy cash flow, you can maximize your business's while safeguarding your personal finances. Remember, credit should be seen as a valuable tool that enables long-term growth and success rather than a temporary fix for immediate financial constraints.

Here are 5 ways a credit score is calculated; you start with a 300-credit score but you can build and maximize your score to an 850:

1. Payment History 192.5 Points (on-time payments)
2. Credit Utilization 165 Points (use less than 8% of the limit)
3. Credit History 82.5 Points (how long you had accounts)
4. Credit File Mix 55 Points (credit card, mortgage, auto, personal loan, student loan) mix of accounts
5. New Credit Accounts 55 Points (newly Open accounts)

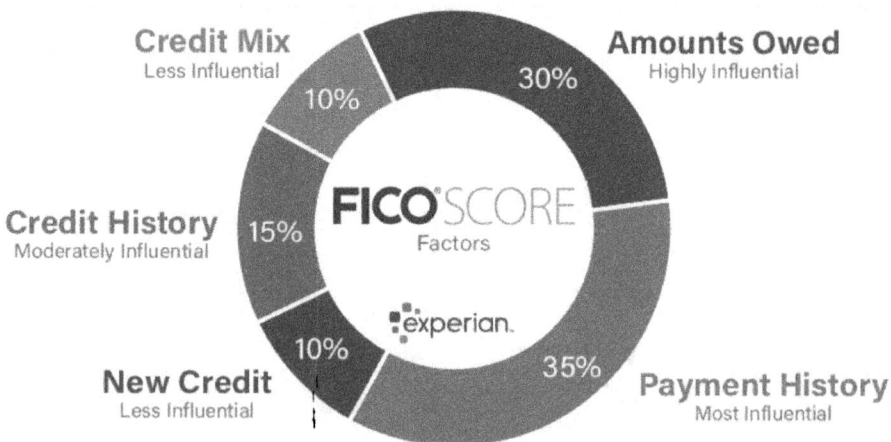

Notes

Notes

Chapter 12

Establish Your "Why?"

When it comes to the world of business, I used to believe that money was the primary driving force for individuals. The allure of making six figures, earning millions of dollars, or living a life of luxury seemed like the ultimate dream.

However, I came to realize that if someone has never experienced or tasted that level of financial success, it becomes challenging for them to truly aspire to it. How can someone yearn for something they have never felt or known?

This realization led me to question why so many people lack motivation, even when shown the formula for financial success. Why do they seem unmotivated or prone to quitting? It almost seems as if they choose to remain in their current circumstances, embracing the struggles they face rather than stepping into the realm of what they could become.

The underlying reason for this lack of motivation is often their failure to tap into their "why." They haven't identified their true purpose or the reasons that push them to take action.

In many cases, their motivation stems from a reaction to what they are fed up with or tired of in their lives. I have observed that individuals who are genuinely tired of their situation are more likely to become successful.

Paradoxically, those who complain the most about their circumstances and face the most significant challenges, such as financial struggles, being broke, or falling behind on bills, are often the least motivated to seize an opportunity.

It may seem counterintuitive, but the ones who are already financially stable or do not necessarily need the money are often the most motivated and driven. How can someone who seemingly lacks any pressing need be more motivated to succeed than someone who has been struggling their entire life?

The answer is simple. Often, the reasons that have kept struggling individuals in their current situation are the same reasons that prevent them from excelling in a new business venture. The factors that caused their failures in the past are likely to hinder their success in your business or opportunity.

Therefore, it is crucial not to rely solely on the allure of money and opportunity to drive someone to change their circumstances.

They must already possess the internal motivation and determination to effect change in their lives.

No matter how strong of a mentor or leader you are, if someone's mind is not made up or if they lack the motivation and desire to change and improve their situation, they will not achieve significant success.

This is why it is essential to identify your own "why" before recruiting others or attempting to inspire and motivate them. Understanding your motivations and desires enables you to connect with others on a deeper level and discover what truly drives them.

There are four key driving factors that push individuals toward success.

1. **Purpose** - Some people are driven by a sense of mission and a desire to give back to the community or leave a lasting legacy. They are excited about making a name for themselves and making a positive impact.

2. **Competition** - Some individuals come alive when faced with a challenge or the opportunity to prove others wrong. They thrive on being the best and want to outperform their competitors.

3. **Lifestyle** - Many people are motivated by material possessions, fame, recognition, luxury cars, designer

clothing, exotic travel, and other elements that contribute to a lavish lifestyle.

4. **Task and Goal Orientation** - Some individuals are driven by the satisfaction of accomplishing tasks and achieving goals. They are natural overachievers who strive for excellence in everything they do. Some individuals are motivated by a structured environment with clear goals and targets. They thrive when they have specific tasks to complete and quantifiable results to achieve.

To effectively motivate and tap into someone's "why," it is crucial to understand what truly drives them. What wakes them up at night? What ignites their passion and propels them from 0 to 60?

Motivating someone with the wrong incentives or goals that are not important to them will yield minimal results. Therefore, it is essential to identify what the person truly wants. Once you know their desires and motivations, it becomes easier to offer them opportunities that align with their aspirations.

If you find yourself lacking motivation or struggling to take action, it is likely because you haven't discovered a genuine "why" that surpasses mere monetary gain. Your "why" must be bigger than money and personal satisfaction.

Once you establish a compelling purpose, you become self-motivated. You don't need external reminders or prompts to stay focused and take action. Your "why" serves as a powerful driving force, propelling you forward toward your goals.

In conclusion, it is crucial to identify and understand the driving factors behind individuals' motivations. When attempting to motivate others or tap into their "why," take the time to uncover what truly drives them. By connecting with their desires and aspirations, you can unleash their potential and witness their determination and dedication.

Remembering your own "why" is equally important, as it sets the foundation for your success and self-motivation. By aligning your goals with your purpose, you can achieve extraordinary results and overcome any obstacles that come your way.

Notes

Notes

Chapter 13

Faith-Based Business with Profit

This is a big one because I often encounter people who have a very difficult time figuring out how to do ministry and business. It's quite simple, depending on what you're doing, I must say. Nonetheless, it's still very simple because the goal is to win people to the ministry to help them. You can easily merge businesses and help others by meeting their needs. Having a faith base business doesn't mean it has to be nonprofit.

God wants all of us to be profitable; He simply wants you to prioritize Him in everything you do. Put Him first in all your endeavors, and your faith-based approach will be profitable.

One important lesson I've learned in my journey is that who I am outside of business should align with who I am expected to be. As Pastor Rashawn Bey in ministry and Pastor Rashawn Bey in business, it's easy to stay true to yourself and be consistent.

It's challenging to remain consistent when you try to be someone different each time. So, when it comes to this, be authentically yourself first and foremost, and let the mission you're pursuing drive your product, service, and income generation.

Infuse the big "Y" of your ministry into the situation and witness God's work. He will provide all the profits you need because you genuinely strive to help people, bring them out, and offer a solution. That's what a team does. That's the essence of this approach.

When you access everything, the reputation of being faith-based is often associated with being poor or barely getting by. However, I firmly believe we are much more than that. We surpass those limited perceptions. Therefore, it's crucial to remember that God wants us to be profitable. We are not just mere overcomers.

Even in the Bible, I noticed that everyone Jesus encountered had their own business. With that in mind, it became evident that merging business and faith was natural. Once you grasp this concept, it's difficult to unlearn it. Merging the two is quite simple because business is about having faith.

In business, you face uncertainty about outcomes and the source of future clients. However, because you have faith, you can accomplish things that may seem impossible but are not. You end up overcoming those challenges.

I also realized that the principles shared by business motivational speakers and the practices they advocate originate from the Bible. That's quite fascinating, isn't it? It indicates that God intended for us to be owners, not merely employees. If you think about it, He always said, "Go to work." He never instructed us to "get a job" or "find someone to work for."

Considering this perspective, it becomes clear that adopting a faith-based approach is not optional.

- » Firstly, the principles stem from the Bible.

- » Secondly, running a business with uncertain income requires faith and belief in its success.

- » Similarly, having the faith to work for yourself is essential. Hence, it's safe to say that a faith-based business is also a profitable one.

Notes

Notes

Chapter 14

Habits to Break

Breaking and establishing habits is a critical aspect of personal and professional development. My studies have revealed that it typically takes 21 days to break a habit, another 21 days to establish a new habit, and an additional 21 days for that habit to become ingrained and truly part of who you are.

This progression resonates with me because I've witnessed firsthand how easy it is to revert to old patterns once you falter in your routine. It emphasizes the importance of long-term commitment and consistency.

When it comes to businesses and other areas where habits have been cultivated over a significant period, the process of breaking, establishing, and mastering becomes even more crucial.

These habits become an integral part of your identity, something you no longer have to consciously think about or be reminded of. They become second nature, effortlessly guiding your actions and decisions.

During the initial 21-day period of breaking old habits, it's vital to address certain behaviors that hinder progress. One such habit is waking up late and lingering in bed, which can set a sluggish tone for the day. Additionally, overcoming the habit of laziness and not following up is paramount.

Waiting for opportunities to fall into your lap without actively pursuing them leads to stagnation. Instead, establishing a routine of consistent follow-ups and proactive communication is key.

Moreover, it's crucial to break the habit of being content with solitude or failing to meet new people. Networking and forging connections are vital for personal and professional growth.

In the same vein, breaking the habit of disorganization is essential. Clutter and disorder can hinder productivity and increase stress levels. Likewise, addressing any harmful habits related to substance abuse, such as drugs or alcohol, is critical. These habits not only throw you off balance but also undermine your focus and overall well-being.

Procrastination and failing to keep your word are additional habits that need to be broken. These character issues can have a detrimental impact on your reputation and hinder progress.

Therefore, it's crucial to confront and overcome these tendencies.

On the other hand, establishing new habits is equally important. This involves focusing on what you are trying to achieve and the obstacles you are determined to overcome.

Making consistent phone calls, striving for tangible results, engaging in productive activities, and following through on commitments are key habits to establish. Practicing and refining your skills and principles are crucial aspects of this process. By embracing the perfect practice, you move closer to mastery.

When establishing new habits, it's vital to align them with your personal style, interests, and motivations. When you are genuinely driven and enthusiastic about a habit, it becomes easier to maintain. It seamlessly integrates into your daily routine and becomes an inherent part of who you are.

The motivation to perform the habit becomes internalized, eliminating the need for external reminders or prompts. When this happens, your reputation reflects your dedication, and others perceive you as someone who has established a strong foundation of positive habits.

Finally, the last 21 days when a habit becomes ingrained and truly a part of your identity, you no longer need to consciously think about it. It becomes a natural and effortless aspect of your life. Planning your day, making phone calls, or engaging in other activities associated with the habit become automatic responses.

Deviating from these habits feels peculiar and unnatural. They become as instinctive as swinging a golf club or throwing a punch, seamlessly integrated into your daily activities.

In conclusion, the process of breaking, establishing, and mastering habits is a transformative journey that requires time, dedication, and perseverance. It is a continual effort to reshape your behaviors and align them with your goals.

By consciously working on these habits and embracing consistency, you can significantly enhance your effectiveness, productivity, and overall success.

Notes

Notes

Chapter 15

Will Power over Skill

In the world of business, many times we tend to seek out individuals who have exceptional skills. We tend to believe that the most successful individuals in business are those who possess superior skills. We are drawn to those who have been sales professionals for several decades, those with extraordinary talent, and a track record of closing deals.

These are the people we typically look for until a realization hit me: individuals with immense skill and talent oftentimes cannot be effectively coached. Their skills are valuable, but they do not inherently accept guidance, wisdom, or direction. Which can become a disaster for a team or organization. Due to their level of expertise, they do not easily receive leadership.

» Skills alone cannot guarantee success if they are not paired with a clear vision and proper guidance. When the mind is not aligned with the skill set, the results can be disastrous.

» Skill alone cannot provide direction, wisdom, or guidance. Skills can only be applied when the mind instructs them to do so. If the mind is misguided or if the actions performed are misplaced, the skill becomes irrelevant.

» Skill without direction is like a ship without a rudder. It may possess the ability to perform impressive tasks, but it lacks the guidance and purpose necessary for true success.

» Skillful individuals often focus solely on themselves, prioritizing their own success over the collective goals of the team.

In such cases, the skill may even make the individual appear to be a loser. Therefore, solely seeking out skillful individuals is not the optimal approach. Skillful people are typically self-employed and tend to prioritize themselves rather than the team as a whole. Furthermore, their skills are often not easily duplicable, making it challenging to build and sustain a cohesive team.

However, there is something that surpasses skill: willpower. Willpower is an extraordinary force that resides within an individual's heart and drives them to achieve their goals. It is a deep-rooted determination that says, "No matter what, I will accomplish this."

» Willpower is an unwavering determination to succeed, regardless of one's current skill level.

» Willpower compels individuals to take action and surpass their own limitations.

» Willpower does not require exceptional skills to excel; it possesses an inner fire that propels you forward.

» Willpower creates an internal drive that is difficult to extinguish.

» Willpower is contagious, it inspires others to push beyond their limits and achieve extraordinary results.

» Willpower is akin to a parent pushing a car with their child's life on the line. That mother will exert every ounce of her strength to move that car, driven by an unwavering belief that she must save her child.

» Individuals with willpower are self-motivated and take the initiative.

When someone possesses willpower, they can build an empire that spans decades. They will outshine others, beat them to appointments, be ahead of the game, and take the initiative. When a person has an unwavering will, they can tap into a different realm of motivation—**one that is rare and powerful!**

Once again, a person with willpower is very contagious. Once established, it spreads like wildfire. It creates momentum, and those around a person with a strong willpower are inspired to rise to new heights.

The strength and determination emanating from them blocks out any obstacles or distractions. They remain laser-focused on their goals, pushing forward with unwavering determination.

In summary, while skills and talent are valuable attributes, they do not necessarily equate to effective leadership, the ability to work within a team, or success.

Willpower, on the other hand is an extraordinary force that can drive individuals to achieve greatness. It surpasses skill and creates an unshakable resolve to overcome challenges and accomplish goals. When harnessed, willpower can inspire others and lead to remarkable achievements.

Notes

Notes

Chapter 16

Five Questions Gets All the Answers

I believe a person who has all the right answers should be celebrated as the most romantic, as they know exactly what to say. However, in reality we have been taught in school that only certain individuals possess this knowledge. But it is the extraordinary individuals who go above and beyond that truly ask the right questions.

When I ask questions, I tailor my approach to get exactly what I want. By asking the right questions, I can find out what my client is looking for and how they want to be convinced. They will tell me if I asked the right questions, just like in an interview or podcast.

Boring podcasts lacks good questions, but the truly impactful ones can draw out the best from the person being interviewed. There is a serious formula for asking questions that can help you obtain anything you want from a person. If you follow this formula, you can achieve success.

The formula consists of five different types of questions arranged in a specific order.

1. **Rapport** - The first step is rapport, where you establish a connection by commenting on something positive, such as complimenting their shoes. This helps build common ground and rapport quickly.

2. **Background Questions** - Then, you move on to background questions, where you dig deeper to understand the person better. For example, you can ask about their profession, how long they have been doing it, and what they enjoy doing for fun. These questions provide information that you can use in the next set of questions. Background questions leads to the impact questions.

3. **Impact Questions** - This is where you ask if something unexpected happens, how would they be affected? For instance, you can inquire about their dissatisfaction with their income and the time spent away

from their family. These questions aim to strike an emotional chord and uncover their motivations.

4. **Feeling Questions** - The following step is the feeling questions, where you ask how they currently feel about their situation. This allows them to express their emotions and reflect on their circumstances.

5. **Solution Questions** - Finally, you move on to the solution question. Here, you present a solution to their problems or challenges. You can ask how they would feel if their situation could be improved and if they would be open to exploring a new solution. This question is designed to lead them to consider your offering and see the benefits it could bring to their life.

As you can see, the questioning process follows a funnel-like structure. Starting with rapport where you gradually delve deeper, gathering information and understanding the person's needs and desires. By asking the right questions in the right sequence, you gain control of the conversation and increase your chances of getting the desired outcome.

When faced with difficult prospects or clients who may bombard you with questions, it's important to maintain control of the conversation. One effective strategy is to answer their questions with questions. By doing so, you shift the focus back to them and maintain your control. For example, if they ask about your company, you can ask where they are from or what they do for a living. This approach helps you regain control and steer the conversation toward your desired outcome.

Asking questions is a powerful tool for problem-solving in any area of life. When you encounter something that you don't know or may not understand, simply start asking questions. Just like in school, where we were taught to use the five W's and one H (who, what, when, where, why, and how) to learn.

Questioning allows you to dissect any problem and find the answers. Don't be discouraged if you don't know the answer initially; keep asking questions, researching, and seeking the information you need to find a solution.

In a recent project, I wanted to build multiple bunk beds in my house, even though I had no prior experience in carpentry. I began by gathering pictures of luxury bunk beds and researching online. I asked myself a series of questions to understand the process:

What tools and materials are required?

How do I assemble the beds?

What are the measurements and specifications?

By conducting thorough research and asking questions, I was able to acquire the necessary knowledge and complete the project successfully.

In conclusion, asking the right questions is a fundamental skill that can help you solve problems, achieve your goals, and control conversations. By mastering the art of questioning and following a structured sequence, you can obtain the answers and outcomes you desire in various aspects of life.

Notes

Notes

Chapter 17

Work on Your Next

One of the reasons we often see people rise to success and then fall is because people become complacent once they achieve their initial goals. This phenomenon can be observed, not only in the entertainment industry where we witness one-hit wonders, but also in the business world. Individuals who set a goal and reach it may lose their drive, determination, and creativity once they feel comfortable with their achievements.

To counteract this, it is crucial to set goals and dreams that are far-reaching and take a lifetime to accomplish. While the ultimate goal may seem distant, along the journey one can celebrate mini milestones and victories.

For example, someone who aims to make six figures should not stop or slow down once they achieve that financial milestone.

Instead, they can focus on a broader mission, such as training or mentoring tens, hundreds, or thousands of individuals, thereby changing lives on a larger scale.

When the focus shifts from personal success to the impact one can make on others, it brings a sense of purpose, passion, and fulfillment. Working for the benefit of others compels individuals to continually develop their skills, think creatively, and remain dedicated. It expands their horizons and allows them to become leaders who guide and inspire others to reach their full potential.

Regardless of the industry or field, every business is ultimately about people. Whether you're directly interacting with customers or indirectly influencing their lives, the essence of your work revolves around addressing the needs, desires, and challenges of others.

Whether you're in the restaurant industry, pharmaceuticals, fitness, real estate, technology, or any other field, your ultimate goal is to impact and serve others in some capacity.

To thrive in this "people-centric" business environment, it is crucial to think several steps ahead and plan your next moves in advance. By mapping out your future steps and continuously developing yourself, you maintain momentum and harness its power.

Momentum is a precious resource that should be respected and cherished, as it can be challenging to regain once lost. Therefore, always strive to be the best version of yourself, anticipate future challenges, and make strategic decisions accordingly.

Many individuals limit their dreams and goals by thinking small and focusing solely on immediate achievements. However, it is essential to dream big and continuously set new goals that challenge and stretch your capabilities.

Too often people stop dreaming after high school, especially when they realize that the careers and degrees they were told to pursue do not align with their desired lifestyles. They settle for merely completing projects or achieving specific milestones, which ultimately leads to a sense of unfulfillment.

To break free from this cycle, one must maintain a mindset of continuous growth and improvement. What brought you success in the past may not be sufficient to propel you to the next level.

Therefore, it is vital to keep working on yourself, acquiring new skills, gaining wisdom, and enhancing your leadership abilities. Success is not a one-time event but an ongoing journey, and in order to sustain it, you must always be evolving and adapting to the changing times.

Businesses and individuals who fail to adapt to evolving trends, technologies, and customer preferences often find themselves left behind. Companies like Toys "R" Us, Blockbuster, and Forever 21 serve as reminders of the importance of embracing change. By planning for longevity, developing new skills, and anticipating obstacles, you position yourself to outlast your competition and weather storms that may come your way.

In conclusion, to avoid falling into complacency and ensure long-term success, it is crucial to set ambitious goals, continuously develop yourself, and plan for the future. By focusing on making a positive impact on others, you can find purpose, passion, and the drive to overcome obstacles.

Embrace change, stay ahead of the curve, and create a legacy that stands the test of time. Remember, it is not the one who starts fast but the one who can endure and thrive in both favorable and challenging times that ultimately succeeds.

Notes

Notes

Chapter 18

Never Forget what it's like making $8hr

This is a significant issue because too often people achieve success in life and forget where they came from. They lose sight of their past struggles and how difficult it was for them. They forget what it's like to make only $8 an hour, the minimum wage.

When you forget, you become less relatable to others, and it's challenging for you to understand why you can't connect and help a diverse range of people. They don't comprehend what you're saying because you speak as if you've never experienced any struggles in your life.

People don't care about your accomplishments. What they want to know is if you genuinely care about them. They seek advice from someone who has gone through similar challenges and can relate to their current struggles.

People want to hear your story and how you overcame obstacles when you were broke. What did you do when you faced hardships, experienced loss, or felt like giving up? How did you navigate through tough times?

If you don't have that relatability, they won't care about your success story or how much money you made, or the big house you acquired. They can't relate to that because they haven't experienced it.

It's not just about you relating to your audience; it's also about them relating to you in some way. They can't relate to being rich because they have never been wealthy. They can't grasp the financial problems you talk about because you earn much more than they do. However, if they can relate to you based on shared struggles, setbacks, vices, or addictions, you can win their trust and support.

The key is to be able to relate to them on all levels. Too often, people attain wealth and start changing. They begin to look down on others and neglect the little things that matter. They become too busy for family gatherings, barbecues, or revisiting the places and people who helped them during their struggles.

They forget their roots, and this is why many fail in business. You **won't** always deal with wealthy clients; your success largely depends on the 80 to 85% of the population that faces financial challenges, lives in Section 8 housing, works minimum wage jobs, and has limited education or a lower mindset.

If you can master helping these individuals and build your success by serving the everyday working person—the blue-collar worker, the employees of dollar stores, Walmart, or the oil field— you will be on the right path. There are more customers like them than the ones with 800 credit scores who are rich and famous.

To build a successful business, always remember to be relatable. Have your personal story ready—not just the story of your success, but also the story of how you almost didn't make it, your background, and the struggles you faced. Clients want to hear this kind of authenticity, as it builds trust and encourages them to do business with you. Aim to reach the next level, make history, and be the greatest!

Remember that everyone, regardless of income level, should have the same thing to say about you: *'That person came through for me, inspired me, took time with me, and went the extra mile to help someone like me.'*

It's not the things that people see that matter the most; it's what happens behind closed doors. Remember, what you do in secret, God will bless openly.

Notes

Notes

Chapter 19

Don't Forget to Give Honor

- » Acknowledging those who gave us our start. n life, there are four specific keys to giving honor to God:
- » Appreciating our family.
- » Finding motivation in those who doubted us.
- » Embracing our own beliefs.

These keys serve as pillars of **gratitude, resilience, and faith** that guide us on our journey to personal growth and fulfillment.

First and foremost, honoring God is a fundamental aspect of our existence. It involves recognizing the divine presence in our lives and expressing gratitude for the blessings we receive.

Honoring God means living with integrity, compassion, and love for others. It entails seeking wisdom and guidance through prayer, meditation, and acts of service. By aligning our actions with our faith, we honor God and contribute to the greater good of humanity.

Along our path, we encounter individuals who have played a significant role in our journey. These are the people who gave us our start, who believed in us, even before we fully realized it ourselves. They are our mentors, teachers, and guides who selflessly invested their time and wisdom to nurture our growth.

Honoring them means acknowledging their impact, expressing gratitude, and paying it forward by becoming mentors to others. It is through their belief in us that we gained the confidence to pursue our dreams and make a difference in the world.

Equally important is the appreciation of our family—the foundation from which we spring forth. Our family members are our constant support system, offering unconditional love, guidance, and encouragement. Honoring our family means showing gratitude for their sacrifices, cherishing the memories created together, and actively participating in their lives.

It also involves fostering strong bonds, demonstrating love and respect, and embracing the values and traditions that have shaped us. By honoring our family, we uphold the connections that bring us strength and nourish our souls.

In our journey, we encounter individuals who doubted our abilities, questioned our aspirations, or failed to see our potential. While it can be disheartening, these encounters can also serve as motivation. Instead of allowing skepticism to deter us, we can choose to harness it as a driving force for personal growth.

Honoring those who didn't believe in us involves proving them wrong through our actions and accomplishments. It means staying committed to our dreams, persevering in the face of adversity, and using their doubt as fuel to propel us forward. By turning their disbelief into motivation, we transcend their limitations and become a testament to the power of resilience and self-belief.

Lastly, honoring our own beliefs is paramount in living an authentic and purposeful life. Our beliefs shape our values, decisions, and actions. They provide a moral compass that guides us on the right path.

Honoring our own beliefs means staying true to ourselves, even in the face of external pressures or conflicting opinions. It involves nurturing our spiritual, mental, and emotional well-being, taking time for self-reflection, and aligning our actions with our deepest convictions. By honoring our beliefs, we cultivate inner peace, live with integrity, and create a positive impact in the world around us.

In conclusion, the keys to giving honor to God, those who gave us our start, our family, and those who doubted us are interwoven threads that form the fabric of a purposeful life.

By honoring God, we recognize the divine presence and strive to live in accordance with our faith. By acknowledging those who believed in us, we express gratitude and become catalysts for others' growth.

By appreciating our family, we cherish the bonds that nurture and support us. By finding motivation in those who doubted us, we turn their skepticism into fuel for personal growth. And by honoring our own beliefs, we live authentically and make a positive impact on the world. These keys unlock the doors to fulfillment, resilience, and the transformational power of honor and gratitude.

Notes

Notes

Daily Affirmation

Today is the beginning of the best day of my life! I believe that every prospect, every appointment, every client, and every prospective business partner shall receive the words that come out of my mouth.

I pray that what I say connects with the hearts of the people, their minds are convinced to say, "Yes!" and that record-breaking deals are happening at this moment.

I pray that I close out this day strong, I close out this week strong, this month will be closed out strong, and this year will close out strong!

Let my thoughts be led by the spirit of God. Even though I don't know what I'm going to say, let what's being said be in Your Perfect Will. I humble myself to not rely on my skill, talent, or ability. Instead, I rely on my belief that whatever is impossible through God is possible.

Today is possible, and for that, I'm celebrating in advance for my victory. The victory that's over my life, my family, my business, and my finances.

Today is the day that I divorce from yesterday because today is a new chapter of my life! I'm encouraged to turn the page, to face the unknown, and to divorce my fears because fear no longer has any power over me!

As I face today, my head will be held up high. My strength will be made in my weakness. My confidence will be at an all-time high, and by the end of today, I will give You the honor and the praise for your answered prayers, your grace and mercy, and the favor that you have placed over my life. Today, I claim it and I finish with it already being done!

www.ingramcontent.com/pod-product-compliance
Lightning Source LLC
Chambersburg PA
CBHW072018110526
44592CB00012B/1357